AUG 1 8 2003	DATE DUE		
OCT 1 6 2003	NOV 28		
DEC 9 2005	MAY 3 0 '13		
DEC 1 9 2005	AUG 2 3		
JUL 0 5			
9 2008			
AUG			
FEB 2			
MAR 2			
SEP 0 8 2009			
JAN 2 0 2010			
NOV 2 8 '12			

101 Facts About

PUPPIES

Please visit our web site at: www.garethstevens.com
For a free color catalog describing Gareth Stevens Publishing's list of high-quality
books and multimedia programs, call 1-800-542-2595 (USA) or 1-800-387-3178
(Canada). Gareth Stevens Publishing's Fax: (414) 332-3567.

Library of Congress Cataloging-in-Publication Data

Barnes, Julia, 1955-
  101 facts about puppies / Julia Barnes. — North American ed.
    p. cm. — (101 facts about pets)
  Includes bibliographical references and index.
  ISBN 0-8368-2890-9 (lib. bdg.)
  1. Puppies—Miscellanea—Juvenile literature. 2. Puppies—Behavior—Miscellanea—
Juvenile literature. [1. Dogs—Miscellanea. 2. Animals—Infancy.] I. Title: One
hundred one facts about puppies. II. Title. III. Series.
  SF426.5.B376 2001
  636.7'07—dc21   2001031058

This North American edition first published in 2001 by
Gareth Stevens Publishing
A World Almanac Education Group Company
330 West Olive Street, Suite 100
Milwaukee, WI 53212 USA

This U.S. edition © 2001 by Gareth Stevens, Inc. Original edition © 2001 by Ringpress Books
Limited. First published by Ringpress Books Limited, P.O. Box 8, Lydney, Gloucestershire,
GL15 4YN, United Kingdom. Additional end matter © 2001 by Gareth Stevens, Inc.

Ringpress Series Editor: Claire Horton-Bussey
Ringpress Designer: Sara Howell
Gareth Stevens Editor: Heidi Sjostrom

Printed in Hong Kong through Printworks Int. Ltd.

2 3 4 5 6 7 8 9 05 04 03 02

101 Facts About

PUPPIES

Julia Barnes

Gareth Stevens Publishing
A WORLD ALMANAC EDUCATION GROUP COMPANY

1 Dogs come in all sizes and shapes. Some are huge and hairy, some are athletic, and some are tiny.

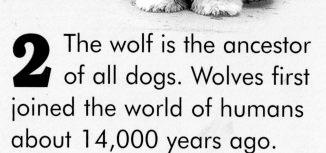

2 The wolf is the ancestor of all dogs. Wolves first joined the world of humans about 14,000 years ago.

3 When wolves first came out of the wild, they may have eaten food scraps left by humans and warned humans of danger. Later on, they were used by humans as workers to guard homes and to hunt or herd animals.

4 To make sure they always had a good supply of workers, humans let dogs with similar skills have babies together. They developed different **breeds**, such as sled-pulling dogs, guard dogs, hunters, trackers, and retrievers.

5 Of course, people later bred dogs to be beautiful, loving companions.

6 There are now hundreds of different **purebred/ pedigree** dogs to choose from. Both parents of a purebred, or pedigree, dog belong to the same breed.

7 Not every dog is a purebred. A dog with parents that have different pedigrees is **crossbred**. For example, its father may be a Labrador Retriever and its mother a Golden Retriever.

8 A **mongrel**, or **mixed breed**, dog is a real combination of breeds with no known pedigree dogs in its background.

9 In the wild, wolves live in groups, or packs, and obey the pack leader's rules.

10 Dogs follow this pattern when they share their lives with human families and obey family members' commands.

11 Puppies are born about 63 days after a male and a female have mated. The number of puppies in a **litter** depends on the breed, but most litters have five to eight pups.

12 Puppies are born with fur, but they cannot see or hear. They can only smell, crawl, and whine.

13 Newborn puppies drink milk from their mother's body. They need no other food for their first two to three weeks.

14 Puppies open their eyes when they are about 10 days old. The eyes are usually pale blue. As a puppy grows, however, its eyes turn dark brown. Some breeds, such as the Siberian Husky, keep their blue eyes.

15 Dogs and people see differently. Dogs do not see colors as well as humans. Also, we think dogs see close objects clearly but cannot see faraway objects well unless they are moving.

16 Puppies can hear when they are two to three weeks old. A dog's hearing is better than a human's. Dogs can hear sounds, such as the family car returning home, from quite a distance away.

17 Newborn puppies make muffled whining sounds and may squeal if they get hurt or separated from the rest of their litter. Puppies usually start to bark when they are two or three weeks old and can hear.

18 A bark can mean different things. For example, a dog gives a warning bark when a stranger approaches, a welcoming bark when a family member returns home, and an excited bark during playtime.

19 A growl is a warning or a threat to people and other animals. It means "leave me alone" or "listen to how fierce I am."

20 No one knows why some dogs howl. Perhaps howling comes from their distant wolf ancestors. Wolves howled together before going off on a hunt.

21 Puppies can smell when they are born, and, as they grow, their sense of smell becomes amazingly powerful. A dog's sense of smell may be a million times better than a human's.

22 Sniffing is how dogs learn about each other. Dogs track smells on the ground and in the air to get information about who or what has been in the area.

23 Puppies start to eat solid foods when they are two or three weeks old. Their **baby teeth** come in at about that time.

24 When puppies are about six weeks old, they are fully **weaned**, which means they no longer drink their mother's milk.

25 A puppy has 28 baby teeth. These teeth will last until the puppy is four to five months old.

26 When the baby teeth fall out, they are replaced by 42 **adult teeth**.

27 When its adult teeth come in, a puppy's gums may be sore. Young dogs usually chew on things a lot at this stage.

28 Dogs have fewer taste buds than humans have, so, at any age, dogs are much better at smelling than at tasting.

29 Although dogs are classified as **carnivores** (meat-eaters), they are really **omnivores**, which means they will eat anything! Some foods, however, are not healthy for dogs. For example, chocolate can be very dangerous to dogs.

30 Most puppies are up on their feet by the time they are three weeks old. Not long after they are able to stand, puppies are running and tumbling, playing with their littermates.

31 Puppies usually stay with their mother, brothers, and sisters until they are about eight weeks old. Then human families can take them home.

32 During their first weeks, puppies learn "doggy manners" from their mother. She corrects them if they play too roughly, and she teaches them that she is the boss.

35 A wagging tail means "I'm happy" or "I want to make friends."

33 Watch puppies play together, and you will see which are bold and brave, easy-going, or timid. Noticing these differences will help you choose the puppy that will fit in best with your family.

34 Dogs use body language to show what they are feeling. If you understand some of the signs, you will know what your dog is thinking.

36 When a dog is trying to look fierce, the hair on its back is raised, and the dog is probably holding its tail high over its back.

37 When a dog holds its tail between its legs and folds its ears back, it is saying "I'm frightened" or "I'm worried."

38 We all know what a snarl looks like. The dog curls up its lips and bares its teeth. A snarl says "Watch out! I might attack!"

39 Don't confuse a snarl with a smile. Some breeds of dogs, such as the Samoyed (above), have a doggy smile that shows their teeth. Smiling is a dog's way of trying to please the person it is with.

40 You can choose a puppy from many different breeds. You should try to find out as much as possible about the puppies you think you like, so you will be able to pick exactly the right breed for you.

41 Size is one of the first things to think about. Standing only about 5 inches (13 centimeters) at the shoulder, a Chihuahua (left) is the smallest pedigree dog breed.

42 If you want a big dog, you need to have plenty of space around the house – both inside and outside. Big dogs mean big dog food bills, too.

43 The tallest breed of dog is the Irish Wolfhound (right) which can stand 30 to 34 inches (76 to 86 cm) at the shoulder.

44 Smaller breeds fit more lifestyles and might be the best choice if you live in an apartment.

45 Small **toy dogs**, such as Yorkshire Terriers, Pomeranians, or Pekingese, are not as strong or sturdy as bigger dogs, so they are not always the best choice for children's pets.

46 Different breeds of dogs need different amounts of exercise. A dog's exercise needs do not always depend on its size. Instead, they depend on what the dog was originally bred to do.

47 Border Collies are athletic dogs and need as much exercise as you can give them. They were bred to run all day, herding sheep. Greyhounds, on the other hand, were bred to chase rabbits with short bursts of speed. They are happy to run a little and relax the rest of the time.

48 Some breeds need owners who have a lot of experience training dogs. Rottweilers and Bull Mastiffs, for example, are wonderful companions, but they are very powerful dogs and are best suited to owners who know how to be firm with them.

49 A dog's fur or hair is called its coat. The coats of some dog breeds need more care than others.

50 The coats of shorthaired dogs, such as Beagles or German Shorthaired Pointers (bottom left), are the easiest to take care of. This type of coat needs only a regular weekly brushing to keep it clean, glossy, and tangle-free.

51 The coats of dogs such as Golden Retrievers or English Springer Spaniels need more care. They have longer hair and **feathering**. The feathering needs to be combed regularly to keep tangles and mats from forming.

54 The coats of some breeds, such as Poodles (below), grow very quickly and need to be clipped often.

52 Keeping longhaired breeds, such as Pekingese (above), looking nice takes a lot of brushing. Without daily grooming, the longhaired coat of an Old English Sheepdog will tangle and mat terribly.

53 Most dogs shed their coats once or twice a year. They need extra grooming during **shedding** to get rid of the dead hair.

55 The most unusual type of coat is the corded coat, which hangs in long, ropelike twists. Both Komondors and Hungarian Pulis have this type of coat.

56 Terrier breeds, such as the Jack Russell (below), do not shed. Their coats must be **hand-stripped** or clipped by a professional groomer to remove the dead hair.

57 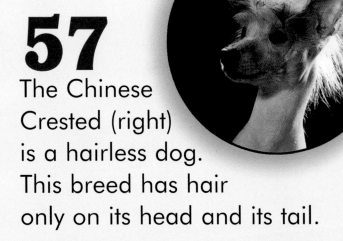 The Chinese Crested (right) is a hairless dog. This breed has hair only on its head and its tail.

58 Different breeds of dogs come in different colors. They also have different markings. Even a single breed can have different colors and markings. When it comes to choosing, it's simply a matter of what you like best!

59 All dogs benefit from an occasional bath – two or three times a year. Some dogs, however, especially dogs that enjoy jumping into mud puddles, may need a bath more often.

60 To give your dog a bath, first brush or comb through its coat. Then wet the dog completely and lather shampoo into its coat. Be careful not to let soap suds get into the dog's eyes. After shampooing, rinse and dry the dog well. Then brush or comb through its coat once more.

61 The most popular dog breed these days is the Labrador Retriever (right), a medium-sized dog with a happy and outgoing personality. It is an ideal family dog.

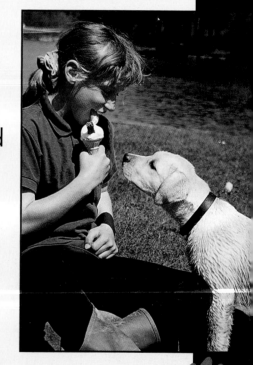

62 Different breeds of dogs have different personalities. Male and female dogs also have different personalities.

64 Puppies do not need a lot of equipment, but you should have certain items before you bring a puppy home.

65 A cardboard box with a cozy blanket makes a good bed for a puppy. It won't matter if the puppy chews the box, and you can get larger boxes as the pup grows.

63 Male dogs are usually bigger than female dogs. Some owners think that male dogs are more loyal companions than female dogs. Others think that females are more gentle than males and more eager to please.

66 For bigger dogs, a hard plastic dog bed lined with a blanket or a towel is comfortable and easy to clean. It is also hard to destroy!

67 A crate can come in handy. If your puppy learns to use the crate as a cozy den to sleep in, you will know the puppy is safe and secure at night, when the family is asleep and the pup is alone.

68 A crate never should be used as a place to put a puppy when it has been naughty. Also, do not leave a puppy in a crate for long periods during the day.

69 Your puppy will need two bowls — one for water and one for food. It will also need a lightweight collar and a leash for early training.

70 Because puppies love to play, providing safe toys for them is very important.

71 Puppies can use toys for chewing, playing games with you, and learning to **retrieve**, or bring things back to you.

72 When you first bring your puppy home, it will feel very lost because it will miss its mother and its littermates. Give your puppy a chance to explore its new home and meet its new family.

73 If you already have a dog at home, be careful that you do not make it feel left out by fussing too much over the new puppy.

74 Soon after you bring home a puppy, you should have it checked by a veterinarian, or animal doctor. This doctor will tell you about the vaccinations your puppy will need to protect it from dangerous diseases and will give you good advice about how to keep your puppy healthy throughout its life.

75 When your puppy is eight weeks old, it will need four meals a day. At first, the pup might not eat all this food, but, before long, it will start wolfing down its meals.

76 As a general rule, a puppy cuts down to three meals a day by the time it is twelve weeks old and two meals a day when it is six months old.

77 Some owners will feed a dog only once a day after it is a year old. Other owners divide that same amount of food into two meals.

78 The amount you should feed your dog depends on its breed, so ask for advice from the dog's breeder or from the pet store or shelter it came from.

79 There are lots of different dog foods to choose from. You can give your dog canned meat or a specially made complete diet, as well as fresh meat and dog biscuits. Ask the breeder, pet store, or shelter which food is best for your dog.

80 As soon as you bring a puppy home, you should start **housebreaking** it.

81 Take the puppy outside often – at least every two hours and, also, after it wakes up, after active play, and after a meal.

82 Try to take the puppy to the same spot each time, then give it a command, such as "do it" or "hurry up."

83 If your puppy has an accident in the house, do not shout. Simply ask an adult to help you clean up the mess and start taking the puppy outside more often, until it learns where it is supposed to go.

84 Another thing to teach your puppy right away is its name. Give the puppy a short, simple name that is easy for it to learn – and easy for you to say!

85 Every time you speak to your puppy, use its name. Give the puppy lots of praise when it pays attention.

86 Most puppies learn their names and the command "no" within a few days.

87 Keep training sessions short and fun. Always end them on a good note, when your puppy has done something that deserves praise.

88 You do not have to shout at a puppy when it is naughty. The tone of your voice is more important than how loud it is.

89 Use a low, firm tone of voice to tell your puppy it has misbehaved. Use a warm, encouraging tone to give praise. Try to sound very excited when you want your puppy to come to you.

90 To train your puppy to sit, hold a treat above its head. As the pup looks up, it will naturally sit down. Say "sit," then give the pup its treat — and lots of praise!

91 You can also give the "sit" command each time you give your puppy food. The pup will quickly learn to sit as soon as you ask it to.

92 Next, you can train your puppy to lay down. When the pup is sitting, lower a treat toward the floor. The puppy will follow the treat with its nose. As it moves into the down position, give the command "down." Then give the puppy the treat as a reward.

93 Your puppy will have to get used to being on a leash, but first, it has to get used to wearing a collar.

94 Put a collar on your puppy, then play a fun game together. The pup will be so busy having a good time playing, it will not worry about having a collar around its neck.

95 The first time you put a leash on your puppy, the pup might object. If you use a treat or a toy for encouragement, the pup will soon learn to walk with you.

96 At times, you will want your puppy to stay in one place. This lesson should be taught in gradual steps. Do not rush your puppy into learning it.

97 Put a leash on your puppy, then say "sit." With the palm of your hand facing the puppy, say "stay." Take one step backward.

Then move toward your puppy again and praise it. After a while, you will be able to take several steps backward. Later, you can try to move even further away.

98 A "recall" is calling your puppy to come back on command. It is a very important lesson.

99 Recall your puppy by using its name and the command "come." Try to sound very excited. When the puppy comes to you, give it a treat and lots of praise.

100 Dogs love to play with toys, so try playing a game in which you throw a toy and teach your puppy to bring the toy back when you say "come."

101 The more you work and play with your puppy, the more fun you will both have. To see how clever your puppy can be, look for a training club near your home and sign up for some classes.

Glossary

adult teeth: the 42 permanent teeth a puppy gets after its baby teeth fall out.

baby teeth: a puppy's first teeth, which last until the puppy is four or five months old.

breeds: the different types of purebred dogs.

carnivores: meat-eating animals.

crossbred: having parents that are each a different pedigree breed.

feathering: patches of longer hair on some breeds of dogs, especially on the legs, tail, or ears.

hand-stripped: pulled out using the fingers and thumb, as dead hair from a dog's coat.

housebreaking: training a puppy to go to the bathroom outdoors.

litter: puppies born at the same time to the same mother.

mongrel/mixed breed: a dog with parents that are a combination of several breeds.

omnivores: animals that eat all different kinds of food, both meat and plants.

purebred/pedigree: having parents that are the same breed.

retrieve: go after something and bring it back to where it came from or where it belongs.

shedding: losing dead hair or fur because new hair is growing in.

toy dogs: very small dogs that were bred to be good companions.

weaned: no longer drinking its mother's milk for food.

More Books to Read

All about Dogs and Puppies
Laura Driscoll
(Grosset & Dunlap)

How to Talk to Your Dog
Jean Craighead George
(HarperCollins Juvenile Books)

Jake: A Labrador Puppy at Work and Play
Robert F. Jones
(Sunburst)

Puppies Carey Scott
(DK Publishing)

Web Sites

American Kennel Club: Kids' Corner
www.akc.org/love/dah/kidskorn/fall00/fall2000_index.html

How to Love Your Dog
www.howtoloveyourdog.com

Puppy Finder
www.puppyfinder.com

To find additional web sites, use a reliable search engine, such as www.yahooligans.com, with one or more of the following keywords: **puppy, puppy care, dogs**.

Index